Disintegration

and Other Poems

Jeff Fort

ATOPON BOOKS

Atopon Books
907 15th Street
Santa Monica, California 90403
United States

Library of Congress Cataloguing-in-Publication data
Names: Fort, Jeff, author.
Title: Disintegration and other poems / Jeff Fort.
Description: Santa Monica, CA: Atopon Books, 2023.
Identifiers: LCCN: 2023944839 | ISBN: 979-8-9866907-8-0 (paperback)
Subjects: LCSH Poetry, Modern--21st Century. | Poetry--American. | Poets--
California--Bay Area. | BISAC POETRY / American / General
Classification: LCC PS3562.D5456 P87 2023 | DDC 813.6--dc23

Cover credits: Glitch distorted geometric shape. Noise destroyed cross logo @ Adobe
Stock / miloje. Vector abstract background texture design, bright poster, banner red
@ Adobe Stock / Stilesta. Folding paper marks @ Adobe Stock / Simon

Printed in the United States of America

Contents

Opening
(phenomenology of finite resources)

another lagging lunch

           rice cooks

                on low
                  [lowest]

                      maximum time possib.   so

     no
loose-lidded spill-

          over

                Odd Rhyme

                    of soft-bubbl'd

                        pap
        and   dense   unseasoned
                cloud   of   covered   summer

day   (no innocent weather now, no simple soups)

An old stew-sapped broth
            sits cold   [slowest]

                        — would-be trash in hand-broke bowl —

        enlivened now   (nuked as it were)   by typing
                                    [everyday alchemies]

All this:

                    sub-particles   3-D now   [uncondensed]

        let speak   here   *what*
                                        and show
        if anthg
                    can be done

with so little —

                    Slow-lifted lid   who knows who stirs

I

A Day's Challenge Like a Broom

I am
Not taking anything
                    out
or putting anything back
                    in   here   Nested

I   am
        blinking

Next to bed is book and so it
        stays   read
                                unread
Might as well   take naked   morning
                                instead
and wind as wire into   sinking   uprise
                        a thinking   kind of
                                    thread

a manoeuvre

. Just finding out there

                                   a name

as in a pocket

                        of empty   hand

        — particul's pulvered out in calc of stick-snapped day
                [evrdy lif$_e$ (x) neo-lib'dearth (>) evn in drms] —

                                so that forth

may come   likewise   and partial   shorn

                        places   merely   shunted

                smile of stone

and odd slip of step

feet now   flat on floor   side by side   unworking mysteries

                                        — to wit that —

"waking is sleeping and sleeping a kind of _____ ."

Cloud

Are rising once again.
Are. Great weather awaits.
Baffle sound into fire-sap,
bribe-write new section home – –
in as or   x – – no more
no sky no school   up in it
Says Jes. & yes he says it so – –   Bullets, hail. – –
standing awkward   at the board
when anguish comes when lessons
lessen packs through cloud and
chalk. Be done, but don't. I shall
live it now. & you shall know – – and
nothing for it. Hover thereto. Himwhomever. *À biffer.*
Taste all until unfine & suture clot.
Erase and witness, love even, remit
Brace and stain, recede aghast
into spirit   & loss, into lineament
into end and end and end and end

fragment
(middle voice)

... childhood peace and calm and unangry parents and a house without yelling or breaking or dying. Knock knock. Go ahead and move in. Summer comes to those who know eternity in the image of _____ , in the image of the senses . . .

Grenade

Brilliant instrument   and over-glass
but still   a sharply sliced way of stalling   &   ticking.

Storage. A major problem in every materialist
   future.   Alongside
  those
of haircuts and bad vision. And how to supply
                              the cavity scooped by paradise.

The problem
of getting up   in the morning, again, pay or no pay.
(Alliterate the series . . . analphabet the elements)

There is a pomegranate (sp.?) on the table.
Knives clinging   magnetized

to the wall.
Fortunately
all this promise of system

betokens (gr.?) as well
the dissolution of   stuck and   sticking,
the menace of endless preparatifs.

Broken grains   but this time
let's call it   splat. A Bowl.
Or something shining and
re-invertible (rh.?).
Something shovable, -elovable
into spoon and mouth.

The glue of it all? The pithy white dividers
          wide road visible
          only from above ?

Ask the ants, slave over their pseudo-
wisdom (ex.?) - - (every

eternity   is subject
to erosion).

Ride greyly into cumulation

and cost - -
be in living   but not of it

In Memorium to - -
no where of ? - - this planet - -

pronounce esthetician (mod.?) - - blink a
cosmos   maybe - -

for only heaven knows what
after this
will ride an eye into
its waiting blade

or an image (no.?)
into unhinged
permanence

Home

Sliding glass reflections
Miniature waving out by the patio
We have these points of reference   a
nice piece of metal   already rust-bound
a dome over coals   -fact is   how-
ever you all   never really did that
Sort of thing   Sun on always-curtained win-
dows   it's the rule somehow   little
turds from the kittens   now   how
'd they get out here   soon enough   a bloody furry
mess   in   the   driveway   Poor thing
no way to get ahead in this   world
or   yes   yes there is   how about try
to stay   alive   and then mewl out
some scrawny   reason   for it   Well Bless his   little
heart   he didn't know any better   all
by hisself out   there   (mumbling
                              mumbling)   till

we stopped trying to listen   ~~Dear~~ Skywardly Father

the oilstain's deeper'n Jesus's
sandal print
&
the dishwa̲sher was just
too loud

Try'n ask 'n see where that'll
get you

Was he the one who made it
up?

(The bus pulls away
till   next time)

Now   the song they're playing   still
cries its peach-fuzz tears

("out on Chapman Highway")

the weightless   ton of them

and the reasons they crave

for being dead already and   calling it

a day

Some Rubrics

Fiction   Fact.

    The Irascibles

    The Provenance

    Flight Risk

    ~~Turbine~~

    When You Came

    It's Me / You Know [invrt?]

    Trick Shot

    Watchworks

    The Grievers

    Grant and Eddy

    Suddenly Another

    Stop Signs

    Last Stand on Pill Hill

Highway

Memorious and sunstruck
this late morning of traffic
and billboarded Dojo. Why is it   Monterey
efflorescing now   in midst of welling wait ?
Why so bright and avenued? Might as well
ask, and answ. (out of reflection (as in) out of gas)   its geometry
but in hologrammatic sense   of totalized figure and dim light sockt.
when what want & known   amount   much rather
to someth. never quite named.   Penumbral sun of all
gone before.   E.g. Euclid Ave. & back-porch Tamara
but no cabin there either, no path, no   [unshelled dates
                                                crunching under tires'
memorial. Pass it passing   & redwood lean. Someth. on
the lawn. Someth. at lunch. A curve over oceanic
chasm. Note : didn't even grow up there.   No way
to make this
public. //   Yet fry down to what gives.

So.

California brings me
here. Calif. called and hung up
a life   it would have been mine   it is &despite
Reckn. with that Hwy One
Count on dying here count on death   too dead   Brother too   [San D.'
at the end of it. So there I will have caught up.   Prisoner? Of sun &
madness so film & filmily out of reach.   Mem-
brane. Manque of more than Madeleine,   our twisted cedrous
neighbor. Morrow for tube of bone & ride till crash?
Planked ever farther   too many empty classrooms &   Lacoue
          too is dead,   that unfamous forehead   [caesura'd in solar madness'
What's the story here?   Is & Isn't   is one
of them. Even after the earthquake   statued calendars "before my time"
                                    Ancient animal print of sweater   but not
not extinct. Africa & Asia. Plain & Savana sic. Roughhouse scramble still
          invades our thermal tissue   this corner of Nickel and Sun

* * *

Wander but through & touch   almost nothing
touches you . Head lashed by noon of it. Steel
trap. Freest Assoc. you could ever   hope
to join   anwy. & sever or sewer   in equiv.

& enchainment & long to gather but
strains to bury when unearthed is
but art's & art's art chalked into
segm. &   poorly pasted layers   //

but through finger   air   why bother even mention
mind. Crook of pernicious ideal, ideal of eat
& compleat? Nothing ever quite zero / but then consec.

conseq.

falling awry of cut trees & ego eatery.   As now as I
sit over coffee.   Sustenance got wher ever imag.   landed (obj.).
Nothing ever but obtrus and obus. Bathroom

door. Sugared lino to sweep. //

Yes blindest dark you could ever hope in.
& so much money passing through   number & wallet
of Amer. & rico   what a name. Alligator   & Puma & maculate Gir.
No mess no clean-up . You do it. Or whoever
cares = why again & this my Cali. & can't &   hasn't &
fumigate. Buy a few more years so finally it
can &yet won't? Withdr. to Blvd. Retire to
Beverage. Die soon enough. When it is you
is ready is gone.

Ow ow ow ow. Ow.

Let go of my stack   & when behind

  & walking and Hwy 5   still has a few more

shots. Turbine yes & Jesus all the way to the 80 from here. Guess who it will really

be, oh Golden One. To save us.   Good to know   it but

Guess what doesn't help. Rings don't fit.

Scratch   and walk.   Go home no

more.   Eventually feed   & release again.   Charred

carn.   &   wait for next time. = One year?   = steps reconcile (subj.)

but do not rhyme.   Could stay here forever.   In this grape-lined field.

The heaven of all this. Parch-grass rustl.
                of unmeant prayer   summer-seeded
                                                           into furrowed weeds.

Hot Chocolate

It is easy to write poems
that don't make any sense,
  said the poet
  on the radio
to the huge crowd   filling all the seats   pre-taped transmission
                    how rich to fill the seats!   (how very not easy)

So still then —
it is easy to. With an ease that skates
through
an ease that loses, in this hand, the next - -
and that notes its easiness
with alarm
and pulse, dwindling   tempo

that piles and plies, waves (he means
weaves, she means weft) and plethora
and delving bit - -

but how do you do it   make meaning
and   unmaking
the line and something
both asymptotic   and

symptomatic   w/o sign or   phone   (keep listening)
        [nucleus too ?   roil of voiced   ATTN!   hands of water]
but who's reading whose reading
it's all a matter of   [blank resources
a matter
of time   a curving and dropping off
                oh nature   [forged inessentials
gross legibilities   fighting for darkness
        and sap ?   stuttered
nonsense peaks toward flat pictures   [eraser smudge
        and movies ?
heart hobbles but cannot quite break ?   [ballooning
after all.   Pity.
Type of trying.   To say
and not it.   Though love is   there-
                                                there
                                                of
In the left and leaving

this strange sense this egg   or
the *chick peas popping* in the water
                    bowl
the nothing-something of such an un-Thing

tyrannical gestures of a freedom way out
                    past
the torture that makes it so   way out
                    past
the alternating vowels   and a morning's
                    demise
that these all   newly left in, unexceptional, opaque as numbered coloring books.

Put it off.
         Pop.   Pop.

Pretend they mean
      Face the gauze that gives them
  over there.   Germane and fruitful.
          Not behind but as.

Soft-woven -sounding surfaces

Now it is foaming . Now it hurts .
Tastes bad . Singles out silence .   Now
    it is time to brush your teeth   Child

Child   what do you   reckon
        they got in store for you ?

More than milk   not   yet   soup
            range of spaces   o   o   o   a   e

    goes down   sweet

                                so   dark   and rich

Nightwalk

Entering a new epoch
when the demand for pleasure
counts too much   too little
on its hands and feet
     a coercive desublimation (step step step)
     balanced between it
     and the old headaches
when life is a burden a burden even
for the young   here to learn   and yet
who now understand   as I know   having asked
what it means   would mean
to be "liberated from life"
and free of this weight
that attaches
to the time
of a merciless and unremittingly responsible
     way of living

* * *

Traquenard and lathe
is how you might've
                    said it
back when pure angles had substance
but is there any true freedom
in words
of this sort?
Sure sure   but what I mean is
how when chained together
the days
the days

* * *

Dense node in breath and seam
                    recur and   recreant
catching but not holding the next
after that   and then
some kind of stutter   still
and then the city that has meant the most to us
and then the corner you turn   toward the least to be seen   of

street and light   and then the night that folds and clicks shut
behind   arched back
and then   there is no stopping no stopping after that

Post Lapsus

months later…	silence, opaque
And then it gets	it gets
to where you	you see and see
Days chunk by	and then
it gets so bad	it gets
so bad that	so bad that
Even this monu	mental monu-
mighty inertia	mind is over-
overcome at least	come at least
for a spell and	one it lasts ha
if only for a ha	If a min-
ute a couple	a mum of moments
such as crack	ling little gratif
ication to crank	i'd first all around
to see and to	hear and hear and
there you see	and then to crack no loaded gun an

be

a star

nounce it

braid abrush

now not on

stay now a way

heart pounds

plenty through

sure soon enough

if only that

only

open to let it a

banished redo only

ly but instead to

no way too many   after-

narrows rooms a

cracks tell tell as

before die but

or that if only if   burn

if

Autobio: *"Je me love, je me bombe"*

Just striving to be - - what what? - - to be
stupid   in line with all broad evidence
  and to let
this   persistent   over-
whelming /   / condition provide
for long dull pulse of all   to be done - - how
difficult to reach, in   maze of marching circum-
stance,   misspelled inclination,   some
learnt so painful   early - - ("be sure to raise
your hand") - - and clung to as though
life depended   lives   and they did, it did,
or so you stinkers led us to believe. How how
can you say   this is not so, or that speaking
up in   rows, or that placing   hope in science,
or that the protocols of empirical evidence, or that
"the barrenness of this world"   and of the next,
or that reason in its harsh corrosive
beauty did not lay the groundwork if not
for life then for   livelihood   as the

sinister locution has it? One thing we
have never had, at least, is   discipline.
Good news and bad, and to that vague
extent, at least, this dull slow thinking
thing we cling to even more and more
deeply, more easily (much work, no effort)
has always in fact led the lines,
yes, led the lines.   Past pretending
otherwise,   before random humans in rooms
waiting to listen,   tired of the exig. & of systems
& of stack'd positions, tired of claiming to be
right, as though   ever were but did, now
finding the true path lies, period. To
be stupid and to lie, instead, see
the difference ? Stop pretending and
start motioning to the drivers trying to
pass.   And so they do, un-
named   but not unnamable. Problem:
too stupid to pretend   to stop pretending?
It starts with the names, not just the voices we
know so well , bombastic and yet so shy   but the names that make
them make them be. The name   she makes   the

voice and still and yet to be? Not since school started
back then   an eternity   but there you have it. Firey sic un-
commitment   and lazed listening of our own
but don't let that stop   //you as though you   could
ever could've. Just lie and let it grow but
no stories   so far. Like I said: problem. Un-
committed even to that, and all this
legitimate lang. & evenly spaced push to bounds
that would fail it but you know   they call
it publ. & for a reason. Publ. & no publ. & in-
stead the word is rictus, say, or deriv. &
derision or derelict. & only now does the situation
begin to clarify, resolving into some newly laminat.
& formula. The most obv. & so: words not voices
the real love in this room   see. @least until recently. Hence
the shift, in titles and   sequencing.   Sans offspring,
after all. Words and powder and putty or puddy i
guess   it doesn't matter   or madder yes that's it dis-
sociated rumaging,   spell that wrong too,
and   the famous patterns and
schemes not with standing. Burn it. Sure. In-
competence at least   trumps the stubborn crud-

ity of such grasping panic   [   ] for-
get about relinq. & just dammage erect. At least that
will not fail in always failing. So canny it's jarring
in that dim underhum, unless, well, you know what I mean.   To say
Just be punct. & stupd. & then. Not that that unrestrnd will
will get anoone anywhere either, at least. Oh fict.
just work it out ? Are you joking ? Let let let

the stream   decide, the wind will where it will,
and only follow, are you kidding me ? No but
doesn't the sea see that that leaves leaves ? Unbranching. To chalk
the word sediment along a basin and its rhom-
boid idea its bizarreries   such despol-
iation is entirely sufficient except that as
usual i forgot to build it. Pole-vaulting there or
it used to be despite the mossy texture and the disapp-
roval of all interested parasites & thr judges. Desp-
ite dispersal and harsh sunlight on the failed
remnants of actual rebellion i.e. this doing nothing
seen in its accurately rendered aspect of
refusing even to consider playing along except as a
question of ruined taste. Thus you become by far
the best excuse for being you. Pad and bounce.

Se lover se bomber ,   coil inward   bloat out , convex
echoes patterned on withdrawn serration.   Or suddenly
Mint sensation   in the gums, now how'd that get there ? For
this you would give up treasure = _____
                       but for now will meat suffice?   No.   What
I am trying to say is, well, you know, it's all very comp-
licated.   Open windows and the items on display trail away   incong-
ruous and free of sidewalk.   Compense.
Fract. & withdr. & Nestle 5's in 3's.
Borderline delirium in abstr. & orders of
world.   Given over to heartbeat alone I
mean -break but in that case   scored and raw
and profused. Lush ecstasies, a truth of_____ .
After-dream of champagne breakfast in panopt. & rotate, but
post-Judd, so we encounter the slacks as well. No more
wrangling at that level, looking up thorugh trans-
parent floors, back in the day   when
horizontal filing was allowed, a kind of
brilliant pianissimo in the library stacks.   But it wasn't cheap.
Bells x 11 or was it more? The seat that
breathes you. Sitting by the fire one chill
evening we struck upon the idea. Wouldn't
it be lovely. Enervigation. Yes, yes world-wide. But ice-

cicles find frames only from here,   in this place only
this beneath   on which to drip away. Leprosy of
the present peel of time, what if it were
bounded absolutely, say a couple of weeks?
Into what then would you shout, over what
line of domin. & dimin.? Awaiting only only & forget.
And, well, what about death? Too late.   But stop shaking the table
stupid, we know it's you.

                                        Imagine, then, next turn of 999
whenever that is   and its toppled symmetry. Imagin. all over.
Can't won't and final round's to   zero zero point zero
                                        zero zero.

Autumn evening: a walk
(blank address on lyric authenticity)

Five forty-five and we are already under
dusk and brightly scattered aluminia overhead
by now so far from the ocean that the ocean
rings hollow in this coastal climate: where early

evening solitudes and sidewalks and buses lighted
within wire quiet through a gathering-in of dispersed souls?
Please for mood just a heart-rate sufficiently elevated to
call it to work and a thin sky that draws the naked

trees. "The sun having so recently set" one hears
such things unaccompanied. Our astonishment is genuine,
but mild to the point of involuntary iteration at
the slightest sign of winter. Evacuation rather

its name? as the foot-towered bell bongs, very unhelpfully,
across rooftops mapped by us all, or in helio hover, demonstrating

in crystallized pain, a magnification, inferno's halo, earth-
quake's resound, visible yes in rotund voices that usher home

to do something, finally, do something new tonight before
sleep, hours calmly swelling, deep layers minutely displaced:
this frame for things that nobody says, this traffic of polished
paving stones, harbored scars and a harrowed bed no beach can sweep.

Lay this scuttle into it, bottomless homes undrowned still
in waking alarm, where all I mean all is singing to me now.

II

Disintegration
(a murmur)

Two lines a day. At least. Soaring ambition, hewn to circumstance. Some unfit
nonsense and soon no stopping once begun. Arc of swat ill-aimed. Goddam fly!

So reckon with spirit of cumulus and conjunction?   Suddenly
noticing the sky has no corners. Unplanned poetic geometries.

Sight somehow begs I don't know how else to put it for handled mass
some speaking of this in which to sink I guess. Nowhere to put a foot.

Yet islands still. Freedom in the broken shore?   Stonecut masonry
so out of date as to be astronomically desirable. A pittance too shy.

More vastly to ask   can there be first principles?   Drink to the ab-
stractions we stand on, to the hard-turned bolts. Skeined, awaiting.

Staring today rather at the window than out of it. But is there a paradise
into which account can be given regardless? Ages pass.   Youth   dies

intemperate and demanding. On a personal level   I find the
refusal rather idiotic, but idiocy is the motherboard of "song."

Remember how Leonard Cohen lived on an island,   when he was
young when you were young, writing at a typewriter, sitting down!

Exclaim when you find the time. Problem is. Time
leans this way   and that.   Is all there is for today.

This urge will animate I guess once its entrails refold   into
galvanized organ. But always something else in a face?   Del-

ete. So lost at this point (trick of summer now sublated, and those
months all agrain) repressed isn't the word.   Pain too has lost.   Its

edge. Almost seems tolerable. No doubt the reason for staying away so
long. So long. So long Marianne. My ancient Greece,   that little devil.

Otherwise you hide in a fold and I peek at you to see if any suf-
focating is left. Always more than enough,   oh hope.

So many to make up for. Days that is and already. Well no making that
up. Voice is fabricated. Love the decade you just lived.   Like a child.

A child. Turned toward that yes despite despite. Turned
and uncertain but of some good fortune no denying. So!

Voice is fabricated   but persona unborn & free. To take on odd
jobs. Cracked fabrik sic   and texture of melted rehardened anim.

So tired, why so? Fiery evening light creams silver   and rose
through blurred front window. Blankfaced I   moved the furniture around.

Now the cricket outside loud enoufh sic to hear in here &   the door
is closed. Open it sit on top step   look listen > "think"?   Q: Full moon

behind cloud cover   trekked above that layer   dimmed in the
day? or reflected glare of city? Both surely unless no moon tonight

impossible to tell. Impossible to eye   and memory has no ind-
ex. & screen machine there in divination and conduit, save force quit.

Just back to level? Don't call it boring   even if. So far preferable
to lower than level. Tanguage sic & grasping at slippery edge. But not

gripping enough, release. Remember that? Yes and small   mercies
so uneventful and profound as to taint the upper lip of every pool.

About as bad as it gets. So don't exaggerate slash simplify   but
now dilemma is little more than reading versus writing = big din and

all that kommt mit. The weighty brilliance of one's domination by
and of the Other (daytime-wise). Just glory, no power? Just rutted

path drawing on instead of forbidding and this   wonderful expectant
question what's next around every corner. And then?   Too many fis-

sures to amount to much of anything. Thinking in images? Bring'em on   especial.
& when longing for the proper amount of sleep. Yes but it all goes into the mulch

my body longitudinal.

* * *

                    The cricket. Every night. Outside the pulse so quick   and regular
breath-clicks   fast as stop watch.   This rhythm   scopes the comp-

assing space out there. No address.   But to in-tuned ears   strong sembl-
ance of address, otherwise   no need for higher recognition of not one, nicht?

Great layers of falsified real. Equals real enough.   Add a recognition
even higher than that? No just more and more neutral more   and more

compass I guess, even as all afloat in dark sky and calm empty   heart
heart. As it lasts. More and more neutral now but what   could that

even mean? More extremely lodged into some neither-nor? A stretch,
a tenacity. No sense then either   and it is there every night   tic-tic

to tell or   rather emit   or as it were radiate this non-telling, this   flat
whorling beauty of something just happening. And still the question why

they do it. Maybe I'll look it up, when the wifi's fixed or yes   good god
the library.   For what it's worth.   Ancient mounds of grain forming

into circles & waves sculpted handlessly into such pat-
terns. That is the schema for almost everything but not

quite quite yet. Still follows. Eye or center?   No further que-
stions. Just scratching like this   across small blank patch n stop.

Runding out sic previous and preceding or all that now useless hab-
erdashery. Linings & pockets and then all the   other declensions

of infracted time filed into reminiscence > recollection > rememoration
> rejoining remembrance and recall   and then   just little hums

of something akin to spaces and ravens or rooms   & ages strangely
self-contained or seeming so   but not to both of us. So evanescent as

to invite a state of constant swatting   yes but is that a state? Height of
serenity. The difference   between an indexical *trace*   and an indexical

gesture, which may include the presence of a thing and its   own
pointing to something absent, is absent in its turn. Vortex. Some-

thing like a winding staircase shot from below   or from antique sitting-
room but furnished post- or just barely ante-bellum, is what's important,

in this scene. But not   for these   grubbing well-dressed   white people
sitting there in sconce of scheming   analogous less to foxes than otters

always slipping through   surface pores invisible except for   slipping
itself. "The remembered film" reassuringly sequestered   despite all   from

your actual life. Until
higher office.   And a

wager to the effect that these spaces too are after all as real as real as real.
Gosh I'd say a kind of heaven even. Where some grey river gathers.   Ab-

sorb. OK let's get specific. The couches do invite. How then to be indifferent
to the dark? Not yet lifted on a given plate of morning and deep dye of freeze

and really there is no deep in winter. Plan, in the sense of flat ice.   OK but
Q. why it always feels like there is, given this side of sanctified expression =

"dead of" and those chill mornings e.g. of yellow school bus   taking its
gall darned time seemed so utterly unbearably cold but really couldn't've

been that bad (until that is years later = friends all dead). Up at half past six. I
mean now all vagues on verge of imminence sense of near future when you've

finally taken hold of life and well there you go, washing the dish-
es instead. First things and junk mail. It's all in there. Push-ups

& stuff. Time   crusted into its pilot's collar,   flak of covered
routes. The supple leather reins leading you to this   very   spot.

OK but what about jogging? Destroy, by injecting, the surplus.   Raise the body
by force above its dead contingencies,   says the curly headed man in violent sic

spandex tights, for only then will spirit *take*, indeed, and a fortiori the cold well
of solitude.   That word made for me, and yet not I   for it. A tread brisk and

damp in well polished blades of dark. And yet   dear six-pack friend.
Goals and means and all that linear bugaboo.   So hard to let dangle,

like a rope above unknown waters.   Might
as well just stumble into the plot   of gold   the pot of god   just hold on

waiting right there if anywhere I guess. Even its emptiness, this treasure.   From
where I'm sitting. Time to get back to bed? Or whe don't we stop fr now sic   &

period. A cough lasting three weeks gives some measure but   whose counting,
I mean pleasure, I mean who's. And yet so dry up to now, tinny doorbell and cob-

webbed hanky. Announcement, or just moth   wings?   The space your in is full
of battery crystals and pops of ear and envelope liner and felt tips and yes you got me

there clever devil, it *is* mean and you're your own best lie. Salvific details in the clut-
ter of apprehension   and the need to shave something. You're neither   here

nor there's pretty
much the sense of it.

But why is it that when the note on the wall says "check oil"
the most that comes of it   is a colored swatch of mere   existence, erstwhile ek-

stasis, in pink puncture of thumbtack? No thumb needed   means drove of ambi-
guity. Floating   contourless over the nearby lake we've been to maybe once at

most if that (ridden so far) that creepy cloud of bitumen   will never find   its
home because it is now the sign of all rhythms' liquidation in the priorities of time

management. Could orb it into dank contemplation? Once at most! though less would
somehow not be none. So ingrained in this place   is the seeding bed (in the knotty

wood) (in the record grooves) (in the CD iris) (in the petals   and
peddles & pedals & pettles)   (in the grit of all we've been through

lately) (in the gristle of teeth and twine) that reproduction is merely that:
an assertion of what is. Propositional logic? Well sure, in a way, but from

where does this tic get the silent gap that insists: no I am not interest-
ed in your unrespondent images? not to mention all that thick sticky stuff found

there where none should be and to which when stabbed with pencil say no Foley artist
could ever do justice? Not to mention its never drying,   its threat of post facto. Not to

mention its destiny as garbage, just like all this all this bland and useful   landscape.
There is no defense, let's face it, from the hills eating pox hmm   what's the plural

of pox   or is it the other way around? Okay it is faced,   and cratered. Even so
the big question asserts and corrodes I mean questions mutatis etc. Me banal,

you plain. And the grapes   float just out of reach & bob, but no diving board for that, much too oral. Rather has it been told through the spokes simple and true. Vibrophane...

* * *

Two by two into the ark   but this one be not bankable anywhere other than the high waters of all-is-finished and whelmed-us-under all you bleeding sods.   The

rest is just hair-loss and fornication and the   irresistable draw of your highly sugg-estible state   of mind and all its endless commodities. Errant influencers have plugg-

ed in. It is tempting to apply. But for now your covert poetry drones away, Mr. President, and we keep   the silent protocol   for such goings-on. Kill List

is the name of the opening band   which is not exactly what I had in mind.   What exactly   I had in mind is that the best foot to get off on is not a foot at all but a formula

for instantaneous conversion. Thirteen point two and counting   every interval in between. Such passions of reason and schema will   carry you far

Uncle Charlie. But for him   the word I meant to use was
pantaphobia   or is it panto-?   The closest we come to that

around here is an hour in the back yard (no snow) and
the renewed certainty of growing old   in the shadow

of the restart button. And yes,   it does have a shadow,   so please just
fuck off.   At least that much, for my sake. Because it is unheard of pain

and merely faltering bursts or swings more like swings I guess
or slides,   slides upward in a way, a   sensation more   graphic

than bodily   merely all that   when otherwise what you'd
expect have grown used to expecting was the clear-lunged [sp?]

call to follow in a day or so.   Heavens, how can you be so
slight in your iceberg of an eye for danger? Downright anti-

theatrical. Or rather have been.   Today that is mostly over.   Today
your memory is a murmur of numb, of number. No, that is incorrect.   Today

is ninety degrees. From yesterday?   Or is it just the strained arc
of tomorrow's nomenclature? It is. But then today   takes a box

of itself to the city dump nka the "land" "fill." Too complicated to inv-
entory   it suffices to darken or obviate   in shapes partially preserved

in principle at least from this bright brass of origins. Today the paint is properly
disposed of. But what then was sheer possibility is now   an integral   part of

the basic educational program.   What will you do *alors*   with all this eternity?
Sunshine burned in as if nowhere manifest. Or long iffy transit. Dead brother's picture

on the table. A child's sudden passion for knitting, daisies and yarn.   both
a legitimate prehense I guess sic. The woods by the lake, there too we went long

ago but only once = infinitized inter-reflection of surfaces   cavelling off into endless un-
dress. Such meager stuff. But surely that is the wrong word. & just as surely there is   no

such thing. Bleating saxophone please say something different, one house over. Mary had
a Mary had a   chance to make it snow. But lessons are expensive and   it's hard to con-

centrate, most days, especially now in turmoil of invisible   menace, but
back then there was not even any question of such totalities, of unfolding

such a long game into who knows what mass accretion. Dead brother,   it's your
birthday, and then your dead-day, to-day, as it used to be, and mine comes right

in its Wake. So born decis. Death as dull invigilance to memory   of departed? Yes.
And so dim tug and current   along all these   untasked days.

And then   drinking alone at night   or not alone   how much
could that matter just something to cut through the funk in the gut

after all that garlic bread. No way.   No way dude. No way to remember much
of any of that.   Consider   last night   the bottle of whisky left behind   by

a departed friend's (bitter) ex-   so worn out by our empire and its append-
ages he preferred to return to the nation without a state, to live out the strait-

ened years. We don't care he said whether 1 state or 2   we just want to be
free.   All this

and another couche since that was not last night but a decade or more ago
but   seems about the same doesn't it you foreshortened gremlin of a life?

* * *

The question now is whether screen left or screen   right
and whether it makes any difference and   why even say

"screen" when what matters is pure utopia. A Q. of perspect. & the rain   falling so
hard it swerves sideways   winding under this doorway. My gutters, must you

tick-tack at me so? All I want   is to get started finally. Started!
finally. Raked breathing and pulver like this leads to the conseq's

we know well   along with all the other interrog's peculiar-
ly designed for the bed-ridden night-hackers and their ear-

ringing mysteries, oh Cuba. As in first what's there   and sec-
ond where exactly does the prism bend?   And if the master

metaphor is shatter not inflection then how even to how even
to how even to oops finger stuck   conceive or set down any-

where any scratches or leavey scuts   that could heap   and train to-
gether the most minimally evanescent non-thing in the space opened

thereby? Twist unto permanent bent but not quite broke. These dreams,
vocal visitors. These darkened sussurations, lipless   and yet hi-volume,

so distinct yet flayed of all   that could pick up or be laid
to rest outside. Rain you soothe and besot me   bedside lead

of sky, you figure even here in the phone's alert   the min-
eral conditions of all our contact and contacts. Outcutting our

unproductive clouds as on most upcast days   in these parts
lumbering into big wide socks tightly strung for that purpose.

But when I say drain I mean empty gorge of deep-sighed   vibr.
that again & naturally we would have it so, nat'ly it is given in strut of noth.

* * *

Glow then, and glom, the wilder methods having been   abandoned
but not superseded   seasoned I guess   with kindness and wind

and mild meat of hind, wounded round of mildew & remedial widgets attached to
the glitches. But there precisely is the 'brasion. No effacement without mark there-

of. No arch of access meeting in heart-shape sign of drip & do-
without in untoward foregrounding of chosen drug we all inv-

essel, whether beliebig or not. Obsession with *that* a grossly stellar indic. But of what
if not a rising phenomenon of intertwined systems. To reckon   on our weather.

I wonder though   when the steam-train will arrive   and the kindly   spindly
keeper of it and the pass of miniature vistas and the yellow coupons & so odd how

some insist it rhymes with scoopin's. Untilled   culverts cut beneath the rise and over-
pass from which to comb through the   scrub.   Visually I mean, you filthy wiseacre.

* * *

* * *

I love the warm fall time. When   dried and clear it lets   brown in
and not just panting cracks. Wist of thick air? A second breath in the

branching reach of double-coat exposure to   all the grinning
meshy screens. The meteor   and the little store on the corner

and the whispered city-shape of things   in hours   of half-dark
after sleeping or rather   waking I guess that'd be.   Re-sigh

and roll over? It's all in the position   and the thing you press   your ear
against. Globed dominion of Insomnia. And all the rage of unchanging years when

something like nobility   slabbed its way under   the rest
of it   reduced to striving, mere striving, dried leaf in summer sun

But unlike the rest   not dead yet. . .   So
what?   so what's dead is what's left to die on,

that's what. A withering thingy crawled   into craving,
more gamut than punctum and yet so persistent and unyielding in

panops and unguents that not even any   scabs any
more   not even a cicatrice. Just time for a haircut—

eternally unparted seas—and it all starts again
but mostly by refusing except where truly just

can't. Which = all the time, so problem solved in a way. So   many things
left, really, to observe on this life-sized ensemble of planes and recessions

and yet really, really all that? Yes and no.   November doesn't do it
but just barely.   The real   problem must have a differently insuff-

icient formulation   but there it is as always, the lay of a jumbled cast.
The time of sick trips and a tongue literally tied (circa circus) to unsucc-

ulent silences cut and dessic. & stained   with implac. &
arom. & neutr. as in sarcoph. & crumble at desert edge of wood

= littoral. *Lisière*, legibility of shadow's correspondent rim.   And then   there's
the violence pocked into half-buried remnants. From bombardment to rebuild in

no time flat. Stranger yet is that even dust leverages "the" in-between.
Stays there   and takes,   lets be taken,   in hand before the next pile

is driven, before stalls and repeats. The reasons?   A false trail   but we   will fray at
least half-way through so hold on. No beyond but so many markers along dry rot circumf.

so many heavens to brillo and to cede   into all the appropriate laps of encircuited
progress just DON'T call it torture this luxurious bodily map of our   triumph.

* * *

Could it be that the scattered blur

                                will snap into sharpness by force of some calamity? Can-

cer my cousin, my lucky break? Car crash you mangling rescue wagon? Etc. And   pray
disaster & kneecap this lunatic modernity, this not-even-tragic requirement, for a life so

numb as this at least and ruined already. Ruin the cure of ruination! Goddammitt sic
you piece of shit world, in which we pose such promise & near inevit. & structure of

fate,   such a stupid joke. & we its fuming butt. Still alight in xmas finery & flammable
disguise, that last celebration when we were all still aliv. & repetition means   no treats

this time but poems & pages by the chimney, their turn coming soon.   (Q: does this des-
troy the whole non-edifice   all this ruined time   has been drawing out,   or mightn't

we see there the empty pin's head into which our looming perspective will now   nudge,
meek and sweaty as a camel's nose?)   This sharp nub of love I call it X or poetry for now.

Not because it is beautiful or brilliant or a reflection in any eye ball but because it is
hard, and sharp, and dense as diam. Because, bent stylus, it is something to write with.

* * *

Speaking blasted into prismatic bands, how strange   these sober colors
have a skin, how unlike our histories to unweave the strains pressed into them.

So another problem has to do with exhalation: pressure   and word under it. Further
violence that seems always elsewhere only to those sitting obliquely   in the spheres

of its production. For otherwise the pressure distils its images.   And so it was that
one morning he woke dreaming he was black. As if falling into some   primal lyric

fault. Wondering if this is what it takes to breach the white imagination with   something
other than itself. Could be that gates unguarded open onto loam of coded   allomorphosis.

Or just   poor white mind reaching as if to some   inward rest?
in Innocence of unconscious   angling? A moist and Awk blank here. Too much of

that snowball's little hell. Meaning   too much   calculation
pinned   into tense flesh   and still-pending mountain of   harm.

Calcinated then into something like a heart's hidden errance and meantime.
Just go through it and see how so?   Better lean on both legs and wake in

face of whatever it shines in that direction. And stay all the way   out
in it, said the face-shape in backlit leaves, night-sharpened promissories.

And be careful of ancient dream friends so amused at first. Centrifugal fist as
if no waking. No further waking except into sheaves of interlocked gazes.

Radically new inflection visited upon previously taut play of wiry springs in social matt-
ress. Elective become suppressed and compulsory, simult. & snap here and there, a day-

long bale of tobacco. Harsh chew of what you know, but only because
you know & think you know. With whose body then this knowledge? I

is not just another, but the orphan of a scattered sense of reproduction. A matrix.
I'd give up now, if I hadn't. Already = the point is moot. Already the foam for

some strange reason, the mass of dying bubbles, & the orphan = California.
In pines and premise of presentim. & the cells of home, wherever

you are. Still back there clamming? Rather basket lined with sandy frags. Thing
is, when *you* say the murmur the murmur is still everywhere & crucially

what gives is the register of sorrow and dissipation, right then and there,
precisely right then and there! Pushing on as though to negate and

to ferment were the damp fire of dialogue. The kind that climbs out of sight but as
I say finds itself always just here   I guess and edging   into someone's sensorium

and what we wouldn't forfeit for an image now, that
simple datum,   that straught & sic & fugilant thing.

* * *

Big as night on this mortal earth.   When it too will die = never,
basically.   And so voices turns encircle for now the shell and gas

this mortal-immortal earth. Yet soon enough no longer after all.   As if ever
was. Scratching toward and only to that end.   Except   evrthng sic

& in between what misery. And delight. What misery   & delight
laid low   in broadening specters and width of band. We break it down.   Grain . . .

blunt finer tip of diff. & steel between grade and section.
Which one now and   which one then and how to render

this = an at least partially   irrelevant Q? Or no
just the whole please.   Even if then no telling which pre-

ponderates but by jiminy that is surely not the question ei-
ther. Thing is we don't know. All the way from here to Man-

hattan   and   the thing we don't know   is if is is what is is,
isn't it? From eyebrow to eyebrow but nversly sic keep plucking and by def. & even-

tually you'll sheer it. Can't we just let that be the point: to   clean and
clear and simplify, all the way to unaccountable wrench, a kind of Ozu cry?

Let it R.I.P. he said holding the taped-up remote. Those were
the last days   of that you see because since then you can act-

ually count on one hand   the passages that have self-bent into such
junctures as those to which that blank face bore witness, such stamps

of passion modeled into   schema and music.   Such devastating
palindromes & irreplaceable singularities that al-together & thereby self-disproved.

AKA such devastating abstraction. Your first mistake was thinking you'd need   to
read everything BEFORE. When what is happening since always is that it is all reading

you. And undrstdg that it's that that you really have to read. It's like   chang-
ing the subject when   what you're asking is   for an apology.   Or look

the mosquitos squooshed flat sic on the ceiling.   Can't even
reach that high jumping and with swatter and trap-tape. All the better

for making the impossible point you're trying to get to &
must already have been at   of a late afternoon in summer

those long days that end too soon   and yet pretty much exactly   when
you'd expect. So someone needs a ride somewhere after all, as if that would help.

And the quandary builds. The quarry. Even the old lighthouse is useful
compared. For above all what you don't see   is the landscape in its

totality, this time   not an idea   but a synthetically unified   field
of sensory apprehension and motor activity. The difference? So long and so radically

has this project failed that over a gasoline canister alone   is there more inverted
and breathable air, fumebound and redemptive in its crushing &   outspinning

absence de soi à soi. Transfer mere memory and   more often
and accurately than ever imagined. Might think it a new develop-

ment   but so predigital as to give manual a tri-phalangeal exam.
What it means is   brain. Scratch it and see: crystal case of

pure interruption. Headache and spirit of liquor.   Or just stuf-
fed noodle? We are so Latin and yet so germane.   To conclude: Latinate, germ-

inate, it's all there, see, "in the head"   & yet so   Danish and coffee in
the morning. That's where the karate chop stops and the   poetry begins but

of course these are not exclusive in your newspaper much less in your metric
tons of procrastination Index. Becoming   other and other first   yes of

course but the way there is so much   longer and strewn with rubble
than any drought-risen shoal worth scuttling into. Or even just already

to have been at it. So densely   long and airy that when
a shred of thought takes wind   as of rag on line, well

you better get busy. Carcass and putr.   &/or at least   pumice
weight. As of eyeballs again   starved and cataract.   Squeezing

out last sight of object and last frame of vision the
gel then discarded. Protective add-on or coat aflap

and real thing emerging, left standing but not enough to climb
on   or over.   Arbitr. & obtrus. Chunk and Drag.

Not even a can to schlepp   the precious resolve   but it tries   & tries tires.
Dreamwork, unpaid. Unmoving. Eternally misdistributed. In-lodged rath-

er than folded-up cerebell. Pry it out, foul jammies. To leave undisplayed this
nugget of middle night.   Pure   empty spocket sic.   World of echo &

glowing unhome. So close really, and so little.   Especially when   good
god   never noticed the precise scale   of failure & now so bleeding obv.

when you add it up. And unfortunately dividends don't matter des-
pite the fact that when you're writing you   can evade more or less

silently the problem for example the problem of a translator who
bent before a puzzle must preform confl. & calculate   within that

one square all the movable intersects. & whereas when just you   you
bend scribbling   everything moves   so   incessantly and so indefin-

ably that the best of it is still   but clouds, but clouds. But clouds   de-
ortolate = (I think)   burn dripping and then are gone. Go ahead   blame

the blue tremor or darker still the entumored brain   of night.
Claiming two at a time and revolve but revolve also   & also = verse.

* * *

* * *

Consider: Waking from his creature dreams Kafka   saw himself a black
man. A man   he called Negro   & saw   ascend

to the Angel orders   dipping bell-dome of human   shouts
and was lost like all his brothers in zones of "bring it back" hard

enough to hammer on. As are we   once certain pockets of distance
have been gold-dusted.   But what terrors as of pencil and fire for the

poor   metaphoric   human there transporting   independence &
denying the one who leads the way into   true embodied   steps

of transcendental crisis.   All lost in icy blur of here?   Way out   ahead
nonwhite   knows the snow, and the true order of recapitulation   undone

= renewal and response of simil. in other. And white and black inter alia will be
as of sides of something so close to brown threshold as surface to world in all its

guises, opened to every possible face built and opened faces no longer in common exactly
but both   inscrutable-opaque and   evident as day. Let prose make it so.   Leve it sic

up to this and you shall we shall have made it and made it up. Clear and clouded   and
red   impressed upon the bloody water-mark with which our founding documents must

henceforth be printed. The multitude   not in its unity   which is too steep to
play but in its stark   cracking up. All its stark calling out   of breath

so terrible once called crazy but now just = the news. But now just that red and
what used to be called soil now   just open earth. Once properly called   veins

but now little more than dust and tumble forth   all anonym. & of   such ur-
gent encern to us sic as though of yesterd. Calling end of ends? Or just fizzle more

likely and out but too much real suffering in the offing   cause   can't
you tell   people want war? Until just under it as in just   under-wire.

But no just under. Which is   where the real break begins,   death driving
imagin. & historic rates of return auto-"justified" at that point   those rigid margins.

Mess and nonsense idly demystif. & ynforeseeable intercrossings or is it unwravel sic.
Looks to me like a drug overdose,   that long unattended convulsing on the sidewalk:

Summer bridge over the Seine   rictus-faced watchers
                              black-armbanded agent didn't bother   to wave us on.

* * *

* * *

Vehiculate the strains but now without   the least   "sense
of an ending" much less the grab you thought it'd be   so pull up and

out   before igniting. No tricks. Fuses or *fusées*,   whatever will catch   and
call it a flash of anti-system   can you see it yet? This wet hand in a hooking scrape

of lint and leftover. Ticketmaster and the Silver Cat Cab Company: a pile. There is no
No there, no of. Certainly there would be more than that, to it, if we were really con-

cerned with this inventory and its wide-leggèd tables.   But
the oeuvres are so complètes sic that even our inferior floorbound

digits   have a place   in the spelling.   & our velvet eggs. Credit card ac-
cepted. Limbo Service Available sic. And   all the stuff picked up   while

walking, out walking   unregistered.   Might as well glide slouched
over the latest Device. Might as well tank. Instead   this evaporation, no

return, not now, not for the good of it all or some later sweep and pan. So much
junk and yet so hard to fill the   land-

ing. My for-you says its crust and little more.   And it's the crust
that grows   within, thumbed edge of a thing used to be called con-

science, used to be under the bed, but now around the lip and ready
for one last bite. Keep gnawing.   Eventually you will find out who

they are   all these people in your poems slash pants.   Rudiments, fun-
daments. There is someone. At least as long as no one sprays it.   Sprays

be. The tweezers will find the follicle,   the lashes and the
strap. I'll be right back there now that's much better isn't it.

By half at least.   A stack of language stuff, indisposed and possibly   indecent?
Yes and no. Spiritual automaton? Getting there but not quite   still too   over de-

terminated sic. The undiluted core of atomic dissolution? Warmer.   Something
broken and too ancient or indifferent to figure out what   much   less to fix it?

Bingo. Broke that can't be fixed   because   no unbroke to know.   At
best the shard of best. Dynamo of divots. Shorting circuit thirsty for

pattern. All the while   worried to death at face of time   and the missing charm
of the whole, despite drainage down to all but. And then the politics of precipitation, as

both main point and diverted surface. And then   preceding it   such a face
as a child's drowned among others. Lentillated hand sic posed on foot of dang-

led lynch & dark gangled human hair all implated as of varnish,   like a damned
ashtray you see? Smiling or not   it's exposure time. An emblem, but not exactly.

What I mean is that the world is there, in every sense: meet and meat.
And the time for figuring out the difference is thinner than dead water.

Is there a way to test your hypotheses?   Beloved rowboat of unfals-
ifiability, drive through the foaming spill, couch the siren of your unwav-

ering rigor. Disintegration?   Assumes the integer?   Lately   we have had rather need
of a thinking enucleated of its   enkernelled potencies,   but those bets don't pay   do

they, in that very special hour   to which all roads   lead,   unspoked
and ironized into pure caramel   or no must be taffy.   What I mean

is that this has happened   to thinking and   as naturally
we are unable to think this happening   so are we inapt

to think its recursions   and so hit return.   Leaving us with a ripe
cough falling from sleep   into the order in which it was received.

Programmed from above   if you like   but don't you find that model
by now to be riddled with false inclines   and yet whence   that

figure,   riddled with?   The chair rolls untenanted across
the floor as if.   That's the way it used to be, those days in Brooklyn,

a piece of sporting history   not memory or slander. Too much of all
that already. But the invisible man drinks a gallon and still has that

little problem of his. Only time and skeleton   too calm   to liquefy
or rather to de-superimpose mere covering and spirit's Spring, The End. Un-

mapped networks and   all that stands astride. Striving still and stubbling
onward sic I guess. Reduce   and breathe Arbeit,   swear off rest.   Will

the cancelled hands continue   to show up
in your slang? Time to be afraid? More like mixing

basements   and business. Binge   of electric mixer paste   leftoff-
er   sic again. The dust   again, and its insistence & its questions. The bark

and gash. Hayseed. Hawser. How can we possibly.   Arrhythmia.
Aphase. Until suddenly dawn lies squelched in odd blu-ish band

of fabr. & the specter of our woes, mid-century modish,   bends aghast
into slack rubbery hands   ready for untended watch,   and so that's

it
                                                                    the
                                                              switch is on.

                    * * *

Remnant scrap and stress of herniac seam. The nature of it being   the
being of a being of no nature discernible under categories   and cankers.

Or the thing that obtrudes no longer but in the mode of its horrifying
viscous perversion and a refusal   to resolve into migraines or tacks.

But now that brown brown reality. Still favored by lightless hour &
insomnia?   Not so much   rather a feature say   of the sidewalk

after rain and precinct of unhinged reflection   I mean   spherical one-
time pills to stop twitching and angst. Stabbing at questions   and bro-

ken bulbs galore. Okay but help me now my old learned friends   like you could   back
when I knew you & you all knew why the gaps were there   down the   middle   and

the true meaning of the poetic hymen.   And then   decades later when the favorits sic
among you sold shelf-&-chair—storage of physical objects being both the perfect angle

and the crisis that ruins the placement of any point in empty space   full stop.
Pin the note to the cork and burn it? And how else on the page to get   from white

to black? How to hide   and then show   spectacle of   getting there   from wher-
ever You were born? But let's face it the public's disinterest is vaster & more harmful

than any rage. Disinter. Destinerr. And yet   consider all those success stories in the South:
Id est. They used to call it racist love. As in the principle of an unmeasured razor. But what

about "the now"? That which recapitulates is us, to us. But neither circle   nor straight
line. Just rhymes with white   but isn't, nor is it pious, the lie.   If only you could

help me & this soon-to-be de-programmed machine and all the sense and fall.
Ellipsis. Is not even the word. But we also know that that ache   still

drags on & that that appeal is both a lie already and the   dauntest instir-
pation sic   of specter in the first place & just another fire   already out.

No stopping this? Except precisely   when cannot?   Expel canning and canner
herewith. Liquidat. &   on the inverse too even. Trying to hate thoughts and eat

them? No getting round? No pole. # 3 in the morning   & no
dreams. Britch tailored to this   not to non-sleep & hence no   stop

& no   henceforth at once. So strangely once. So gradually   does the spinning
fan click and blade   from one extreme of arc to the other   so gently

does it rock the coat-hung shirt   the   sheer and useless curtain. So when
lines break the rocks lie there   unworkable roadside. So take hamm. & shatt.

& rage

after all.

* * *

Horse shoe   & unstamped iron. Reticular strettheim
unto blas and blas. What we live in   and must break

out of. To be on the screen at last   the curved outer
surface claiming not reflection but projection and touch

of other-touch in gaze of same. Before   I mean ontologically
prior   to inbreak and outshatter. Ausschatten.   The off-leap

of time into its own trunked tail   dark contour of it and season
change. As though blank were there-at and before   begin of all

by which I mean to follow blackness   and possible outbreak and obf-
uscated ctr.   Q: If white as such has presumed to rule then somehow

is it   yes   that

black were there in very core?

This thinking affecting thinking itself, as light breaks on Gold Coast
as gap breaks into gab and Gift. Black gap of being you   you

Greeks. When beginning came only after and capit. & guillotine
the brume and shift but wave did crest and breaketh not. Blood

and spume & that too of core, of cores. Say this   and drum and score.
When what you really mean is disinstantiation. Turn it off dammit if

you can, once robinet, once Sprache spiked. Thing is   no value or exch-
ange, but EVEN THAT says nothing other. Since hidden   and burning

oh alcohol & spirit   very schema and feel of metaphoric collapse. Single
head even in falling partakes of universal bond & meaning's   sublime de-

declaration & therefore cosm. & spasm of eternal oblivion   but
EVEN THAT does not amount to   oh never mind. Truth is it's

too cold in here, too space and too sense. Truth is   it's a zone
of suffoc. & may stone pile   at and before beginning. Hardware's

false chains of encastration. Truth is it's is that's   used to blanks now.
Despite all and   sans regard. Tree branches   filter light.   Eponymous.

Eraser rubble? a misnomer   clearly. Crackling snakeskin &
path toward retread   writing or traces maimed and so made

permanent. Border of visible, isible.   Corner now wide enough
to maw it in & that emits & emanates.   Hungerlicht   he could've

called it. But he'd've been wrong   to. The hunger is   for end in end &
so is for itself. The thing that starves it   is it. Find that syllab. & go past.

* * *

* * *

What is strange is to be dead, and to know it somehow, without that
nullified sinking into day and wake. Dead   and yet still, to be dead

is not so hard. Persistence sneezes on the sleeve of lazy, and there it is. To
be dead or dead to   =   a Q. I've asked before and have had time to

to puzzle & saw,   as of a complex edge brightly railed through the binding.   Red
this time you could say, but review soon enough. Document de couverture? OK   but

stop spanking the pages closed. Late afternoon and deadest
of all something like the hot toast of memory stoned out of

all relation by the very name it wears. Paris and the gutted curb.
Just keep coming back to   dead and yet   & you'll be fine, she

said, to the kids in curving rows who'd paid to be there,   as though
promising release   of all complication and misunderstanding into

something no grade can measure,   as though saying   *you will have it*
but only if you've gotten it first, as though the skylight   were not a dire

distraction, a picture of brainless being, a tactful lancing of bulbous
certainties,   especially for that   arrogant *phénoménologue* we

keep trying to trick with ice-cold remedies and   universalizable claims
of taste and habit. Yes habit too makes claims, especially post-recidivism.

The foundation of both   climbing & kicking out from beneath   & thereby of
the conditions   of its passive over-coming. To be stuck "with Stupid"   but

lack even the gift of talent or a rope. If I said read I meant it. The posters may
lie   but the movies don't—thank you god—each being its own auto-documentary

and so a passage through funhouse history. Oh Rita you made it   didn't you
into the electrified grid on which we stand. Because   you are good (bonne)

and generous (généreuse) and because   you   take care of   every-
thing, even me, oh disaster. I say this but   I do not say Improvise, there's

a different class for that. All booked at the moment.   What else?   >   In the
sitting room we called it the hammock   she used to rock all day and   mumble. I

too   would sit, and watch. TV on TV off. Lamp lit at 7:30   extinguished at 1.
As though the story were there either way, but of course it is   of course it is!

It takes a strange kind of ornery sumbitch to figure it out,   that's
all. Because   see   she was dead too but didn't know it. Ituit-

ed sic from across the room   this strange   rugous fact   took on
the tender touch of cream-rubbed wrinkles.   Each hand rotating at

once on   opposite   elbow.   I loved her then   even
when   I told her I didn't. That mad elderwoman who—I know, I surmise—

somehow   ruined everything. Everything that is that the elderman
hadn't   already.   But who can cull the blame   and what

on earth would be the point   damage so far gone even then   that
knowing or not knowing amounted only   to more damage. Profiled

in grey on the long highways subsequent. So many times back and
forth. So many radios   to sleep by. So close to dying then but so-

seeming far from dead unlike now   smooth wax of done. As if always.
So then too, across the room,   behind the wheel, in the   freeze

of a life so blank with promise   so catastrophically vacant of all but
brains and hurt. Unlike now   when from all this only hurt to tell, like

carpet or wallpaper. So flattened and deadened as to lie undead.   Dull
tugging of virtue and refusal   so complete as to seem unable to fray.

What was it   what was it i was going to say.   The crumpled line
of signs   and true paranoia meaning   sheer awareness of

the Outside. Our Insignific. & where ears were   so shall inside of lead-lined screen-
curve become. Used to be   tubes in there used to be   a radio   little people inside

yah. The music   doesn't stop now can't   or won't.   Won't.
Won't. Won't. Ever. Never, nevever. Except   in the mouth   of x-

haling oblivion — mix, lap, or spatula fold? A time   and planet where,
yes a time   where, we're all dead   and there is   no one to rem-

ember any of us not even eveven sic mute maw muzzle or   gorge
not even stone-tide sediment. Or ye mayb stone sic   unsurfaced.   Housed

where hard shell a mere membrane of air or just   gas   i
guess. And for whom. Ask it, dust, ask it again, and ripple radii

into a v. diff. kind of mem. & no head or seat   or   recept.
& only depot   only unhomed roaming and all that yes again

again   a radial sweep   a sub-
                                                           stitute.

* * * [_____]

Raking through   through something that appears to   have   to have
to do with time   and register vs.   undercratered   depos. & bare

empty of empties   but what is   this stuff   called   when
call and subseq. & scratch appear   appear only to second   what was

as in   really was? New year's?   No stimulus this time   w/o apost-
asy   means rolled up   into discipline   as discipl.

& discovering   all this   as though   throwing   networks   of nothing forw.
armed   & escrime & ricochet & one to another &   land hard on kneecap   ouch.

* * * [_____]

Abstraction and if. & if that were the problem and the solution   to the
problem. Is & ain't. But bringing so many more than none   remains

next to impossible. So then abstraction   let it be   our day and
its end. In weltering   world,   in bone and soul   misnamed

always misnamed whence time comes to leave.   What's hard
to remember   is that there is no pain   in true oblivion,   no share.

Someone once asked what is your share of sorrow? = what is
that husk and puckered knot of unfreedom and   weft

or that rubberbanded taper of pocket and pebble   I know
it could be anything. The press of it, the   leg of it.   The

bruise of believing something = nothing   matters. So share it
out and what of it. So   no way not to not   not. Bearing that in

mind   makes sense up to a cornered point & shuffle   wearing off, whether
transitive or locomotion, whether this or   through with this. Or is it that

nothing makes sense either & by that yes   I mean   truly no-th sic or rather noth-
everything.   That's it & finally = notheverything. How to go   straight down

into that or otherwise hang a tale   opaquely vesselled core   dissolved beforehand and
yet   pressing mild acid of effacement   vaguely nearing finality   but fully asympto-

tic.   Only then   will it help   but whom and   how?
The New Years tell but little of these unrespondable glooms.

* * * [_____]

Masses of secrecy   a fixing whorl in wet weather   but somehow   something
other than   the private mischief often taken for a stone's forgotten weight.

What I'm wondering about is the way the sun goes down
down and through   coming round where it left

off   but for the naked window and last pill of silver light. Something so dispro-
portionately terrible   radiant   fascinant.   For a newly dull   wit

like this one. Is it true that stupidity   makes   the world
feel round? I don't mean the harsh   arrogant   ignorance

of your enemies. I don't mean the aggression of the trolls and the
haters. I'm thinking instead of what's the word? I'm   wondering

where the files are.   And   in the absence of   perforation   and precedent,
where exactly the sweetness of the long walk begins and how it makes even the dim-

mest sheet of simple daytime into a dire and empty   call-
out, a gentle density, a thing utterly w/o mystery   and yet

a shimmering packet thrown round   every settled & fitting outward sign
—and so   why stammer?   as though   any inside of any thing contra-

vened its utter openness, a   blank and radical availability.
The Q. is how, avlbl. how   & whether,   by dint of this

unharbored spectral talent   which   is nothing other than our profound
machine nature   our technical brilliance in the most simple and basic

senses, might end up being   the raw & corrosive form of our out-
wrung dissipation,   as in a cloud of qualia and chiasmic exchange.

Indelible radius of breakdown. And the sad grime of this particular   all-that's-left.
But what have I   to do   with affirmations?   said   god-forget-his-name.

* * * [_____]

* * * [_____]

Out on the farther reach of that rarely known hum of the   faculties,
some desolate passion   given over to the pure sap of   intelligence.

What calls? I mean if only I'd learned Latin   and read Spinoza and knew
really knew what it means   to put out a philosophy of nature   at the very

point where otherwise disguised it could present itself   as a means
of heaving through every semblance of operant   negativity.   You

know the kind that leads to unbranched attempts at order and   mast-
ery. Instead   do we truly have but images   and shades   and little

more besides = manageable excesses? The thing that inter-
rupts nature is also the thing by which it is known to be

such, which may   or may not bear   on   what it is   "in" its elf-
in elusiveness   but surely we can't do w/o worrying over this bit of sup-

posed   non-access. If only I'd kept up with the flash cards.
Instead of I   say instead. To turn   or squeeze idiot disint-

egration into something like this and continue unknowing   even
whether this or not this.   If only I'd kept reading Keats. And found

in sleep not dumb tired dreams that just want   just want   them-
selves alone, unto dimmest and most precious obliteration, for a

time, but rather but rather. No not speaking of nobility and oh
forgot to say   no limits of understanding even those em-

bracing the fine skin of all outward throbbing   shortfall   in er-
udition and grace   can be said to amount to the sublivity sic   of what

we are coveting here, id est et simulacrum omnia etc.   No
even then   no even if. Only even odd and therefore   infinity.

Without however having earned the least of it   even grain   and
proof of past effort   so just throw yourself on what's left and glut.

Until   then what?   Rhymes snake their way through   fallen
rubble of   unrising edific. & dead sister moans   and movie

ends. To go on is the only rule or reason or   shape of coming
things but it sure the fuck is not enough   is it. Hence   the cruelty

of that final that final unend. Hence death's face "of itself."   There may
even be such a thing but from here it moved out long ago   hence never

will will again   & so on & 4ever I luv you. Thus always our logic   in finality
and refuse. Like   that face. Is there anyone   to see it? Neither of any   knowing

that,   since no seeing but its. Face   fatal   fatality. Followed
by dates and tended as though visited   and locus of token

inwardness. Erinnerung   or Gedächtnis   so little depends on
this   when   sky sinks   this massive lid and disc and coin

                              upon our cemetery heads.

Or here, where the top of the toilet must be raised,   for commodity.
Strange way to call these things we would fain do without   and as I

sit here long trails of a rainty morning sic I swear all   almost all will
come to pass but not least trace of holy or foreseeing word. Only forsake.

No shadow even just even grey. No foresay just mild precipit. & the odd art
of meteorolog. & tinging the charts all rainbow and acqua sic.   How is it

that the snow is so loud, at least when once again you forget its halo'd beam? Stumble forward, but forward it is I guess. There is   something in this   grey pack that

has nothing to do with morning   or with Q's like where'd you get here
from. All this and there's still that fat rumble   back into   hazard &

pain. A bevelled sort of *vrombissement*. Because   somehow back preponderates even over
fut. pain &. To come. Sky-wide calipers   to measure with and wander through   to miss

things like minute hands   and doorknobs   to count through plastic con-
tainers and wrappers and   screwtop condiments.   To like well enough

the respite of a word meant not to direct   lengthwise but to   frame askance   and a
corner   in which to sit   shirt or no shirt   you get the joke and   laugh along.

If there are still such things as corners or if this insensed game   of
unnaming has bisected the angles of non-dialectical time   leaving

us to pump   all seatless and worn   just staring   now through   window &
wall   just breathing. Not even waiting. Not even weeds. Just a full round sweep

of shatter and eye. Because there's nowhere else to go? Last days   of disorg.   &
delight?   Stark boundaries   ahead. Leaving out the best stretchy parts   of

time and tether. Built-in elastic you see   that's what gets things up on
stage. Emerge and withdraw   and   somehow call these   the

same. Pareil to non-pareil as   widget to jib. The lip smacks the
tongue, the gavel sic miscued.   Root is new bone   so tell it square

and leave nothing out. But   how long can this go on   well   forever   that's
the problem but then again   not really which is   the even bigger and awfuller

problem. Or rather the condition   for   the rest   including all
this not ending and unable.   After   the rains the basement dries

out, eventually. Furniture raised onto thin bricks just don't drop the
lighter. Anyway   bills unpaid   leave little else to do, the morning is

long finished for such palavers   and the wildlife retreats into fence-
hedge and culvert. Too quiet   for another chapter. But La-Z-Boy

sadly you do not rock when you are reclined. So   sleep now and saw
through surfaces   the ones that regard you the   screens   of seeping

moss   the come-crusted towels. To   stay alive in pointless dispersal and useless-
ness of speech and breath   it doesn't   pay does it to unjoint   it's not allowed—

mad negligence and unblammable betrayal sic.   Mere negative freedom? Whose   to
know.   Rocket fuel in the buzz of rumor?   More like sticks.   Just don't expect. Don't.

Don't   expect the wringing to make
much   period.   Syntagm of diff. squeezed out long ago just not

at the level of phonation which   is where we dwell now,   now that   X.
And where the price is logged   the one exceeded by newly bleached irr-

elevance   in the age of an even more catastrophic remove of   equi-
valences. Reset wish by now? When hatred of one world or another   seems just-

iciable and all the symbols slip their pizzle   who in their right mind is not prone
to end-times ideation?   No doubt about it   we shall   circle

our way into it   rimmed by forces that consciously self-express   only when the mach. &
means of interp. & co-spir. & psychot. & alt. unbank beg. to overwheelm us so sic.   So

listen

up. & I'll tell you.   It's gonna hit   but no one's readdy sic. Just   keep
a bullet for your   self each of you   you shirkers and miscreants.   Or

anyway write that novel   and make as if   money don't matter. Put
it all in!   Before time comes to run for life   or rather   more

likely live out long days in tarp and scrounge.   Or leave that for
your heirs.   & for theirs.   Has it ever been   more impossible

to garner at whim & share   in well-propped confidence of   avoiding this?
The under-lesson is that human beings do have a collective   hive-like scat-

ter box   and implacable driv. & what   match for that   will be the angels
that await us   they are already here   pointing-irrefut. & mssgs. &   scrim.

& almost   to no effect what-

                                                                        sore ev.

* * * [_____]

* * * [_____]

So I have tried   but tinnitus won't let me. Bracketed
in low corner of "every single time"   the overall

tendency remains one of extraordinary constraint &
freedom at once bound into sleepy suites of act and

thought. But, she says, the key is gesture. And what this
means is that what counts   is that each one be placed

within some degree of separation   in tangential
relation to the side of things   most prone to slip

toward oblivion. Its vasts and crushes. Is that my job then, this spec-
ific gravity   and torque of effacement   in the eyes

of a day too unwitting and open on all sides to re-
tain the least of these flat ecstasies?   No. That is

not the assignment if there is one.   There is not one, of
that there is one. There is rather   a startling and unfor-

givable brake placed   on the things meant to turn togeth-
er or rather an outsized movement encompassing all that

with the slobber of some hunger persisting in before & aft-
er even after the end has revived its extinguished signs of

warning and retreat. The coffee is too strong and lies
in the belly as degustibus in a pipe. Not stopping on

the way to somewhere else   the augemented and then
magnified process   of occlusion   lets seep the secret

and disordered decatenation that used to be called
inner workings   by those who preferred to posit

such rather than to greet you   on your own terms.
These you have dictated clearly enough but to some-

thing resembling more wax than glass or   aluminum tube.
The thing and it almost is one   that you call freedom is no-

ticeable in ways other than close observation of breath.   How-
ever this other   thing that is not one   that you call   money.

(unless that is precisely it   the thing
                          voided core &   realer than real)

Immune to interdiction and nailed right into the
studs. In purview even of black raven and   regen-

eration of parts. Best then may be to throw out
little sprinkles of acid and corrode smiling the

grim pleasures of so-called spirit but incalqued this time
with the   kind of affirmation usually drawn   as through

a straw   from the deep sources of morality   and dream.   So
doing   both good *and* well,   forging best practices, and in the

drain attached to all the refuse runneling   through
human fissures & institutions & speech nonetheless

wasted in noice sic   we keep hitting the crucial tone
of something saved between us   all along the roads

and boardwalks. Soft-serve and subscriber's discounts.
Banished confrontations resurfacing on screens and in

the modest arguments from statistical rarity. Looking   for
a place to stop. Dring water sic through a towel upside down. Horde-sealed

lunch packs with no ex-

                                                piration.

Grounded now all the wheels as of birds and wings. Woods
and weeds and sun so hot that bike tires   burst. Eternal

talk of all we've lived for up to now. But what
fraction will tell how it went back then when

ice broke off in flavors of patina   and iodine?
The Rule will be followed. The eclipse will satisfy

but only those who walk the path of totality, be it
for kids or kinds. The major keys   will rise as

gusts from strenuous pressing   of stone and
board. The leader will emerge and tell you (slab!)

where to put it. And all this unintended   consciousness
is also so much wishing   isn't it? A fiver sic waiting to

break along the same crack that opens the world as such? Sure I know
what you're thinking   there is no direct passage from delirium to play-

field   but as the jungle grows   the shouts   proceed
undiminished in startling forms, finally, of petroleum subvarnish

and bystander participation.   The new voice rises too as
millions murmur into the shelled corpse   of democracy a

little magic still remaining there   a little wish for   bend and
crash and reseat   regardless of real traction   slipping   for

what matters now is taking the temperature and yet   no one
can do that without risk of tarantello spasm or worse   &

without gripping   through sluice and relay   the very thing
that may or may not be a skill   i.e. an inability in the end

to tell any difference while proceeding *nonobstant* as though   settled
into patterned nest of bulging veins   along with unshakable faith that first

known = most likely to be rescued.   Your cypress trees
bend lining the road to the bridge   and across. Desert

grows too   still and always even as   face of it speaks
some new life that somebody's gotta pay for   and will.

What I don't get is how. What I don't get   is how
at least 70% of all traffic is porn. What I don't get is

it   anytime I want.   Rough approximations there-
unto bring all other solutions into sad relief. The belly

of it   and the brains. You could smell your way
from one to the other   but even that method has

fallen into unaccountable disrepute   as genealogy becomes
a question rather of getting an unexpected leg up in the game.

So this   is what happens when you go about your daily
Venice sic in a mood bad enough to peel away   in strips

of light   but not from the things it actually shows to be such.
Los Angeles? Okay sure   but the real problem is out there

past the canals or on some walk by the Spree where bom-
bardments no longer beckon to ruins but   lie buried and

hulled by so many reconstructed steps that the very notion
of cover has taken on the allure of regress and calls, in vain,

for recognition as the true state of all open knowledge.
Yet in this circle   we wait still, for atom,   for knife.

* * *

I keep thinking that every time of things I do   is
the last. A saying farewell as practiced daily w/ exceptions every

coupla years. Even today   with these rainless clouds
and the sense that I'll never be back here ever   again

in this beach-bound numerology   despite no knowing   and all changes
unforeseen. The sand expansed where parking lots would be but they'll think

of that soon enough I guess just like next door where the dog
shits when and where it wants. Blinds down over open doors

& sex voicing through to addressees perched akimbo in hot windows
of their own. Do the waves relate? 'fraid so I have to say   & inevit-

ably it seems that evening would cover this   hairy night.
And yet darkest of all   are these long sips on a bottle

all these second and third takes   and threats of endless
repetition and the uncomfortable certainty that thinking

is never not also tic & tic & tic. So the hooves will have it.
All 4 raised for nonce and secretly thrown to   eternity.

All cries smothered as blinkering memories protrude like
Lincoln's face   on the bottom of a skillet   or   on

the side of a desecrated cliff where museum-bound   we watch an-
other movie but somehow no shadow   overtakes these exterminationist

Generals. Just thrusting now   to one side or another
as the schema-dream takes body once more and aims

at every other eye. Account for that   why don't you. Or
would you rather go on in much the same vein   pickaxe

in belt and firelight brooding   as embered layers flake?
Now that is inspiration—when dawn closes over this place

and nothing left but   nothing left and a kind of after-
ward   waiting to return to the busy heart of city life

alternately   snuffed into this other kind of breath   this be-
lated recuperation and   refuse   in the sense of both   waste

product so-called (happy leftovers) and just won't. Exertion of useless
residue & all that uncanny stuff   is it true life   or just husk & smut

& cluttery space forever? The impossibility of saying where
the pudding fits into the meal   once we've decided   to go

backwards from the middle   is so bewildering as to present no less
of an enigma   and moreover one aimed at each sense   separately.

Hence the eye-rolling (looked like) when asked her name? For the rest
the post-its   are ready   and anyway   I "don't see color" so

let's call things as they are   unless they are not
exactly things but rather closer to   a somber ex-

halation of   disseminated meanings now gathered   into
a falling stack like vinyl records scratching each other into silence.

Ice memory   I think they call it. Extracting a plug
in hopes that the ages of earth be not hoven under.

And so it is time to keep your secrets   and   to deliv-
er them unknown into the murmur that sustains us? *Right at*

the frayed limit of too late. So play please play that until
it crunches into air and signifies finally the unsprung leap

now needed to make it across   no crossing.
Look what it has brought us to then   this absence of a

book   and its unsuspected opening into   the most force-
ful emptiness ever lodged   in language and   composition.

What place for poets in all this tonguing   and *frisson*?
Typists needed. Barring which erect the hungry flames and the

company of winded marshals intent on a rest now   and
biding   so long as their time may tell a final courtesy

but after that no smoking please.

* * *

Weeks and weeks went by   and the porch   still smelled
of vanish sic. I think the air too   fell ill. I think my lungs.

Inveterate sun smacks of something ending right here   in the early
margin sic slant   right into the scatter they are supposed to repair,

oh feathery hour of synthesis. And yet all is awane.   Far more than half
a life   is waiting but even that's beside   the point.   Crepuscule.

Up or down it matters little   but even   beewings   under glass
seem non-sequential   although yeah I'm sure they used to count somehow. Like

yesterday in surge of disbelief   and marvel   at nothing
more than   time and colors   and people in a room looking

at a stranger newly entered.   You see it's raining   and
I just.   Could even that have led to something? Something

through and off the screen   e.g. when there's no more Coke
to drink   and the pain of ending pointlessly   in an ulcer

in a bed   in convergence   of all that gives life and
extracts and refills   at once?   I   I   hazard to say

that   we   we   don't know   we don't know   what?   And I   I
am   for better   or worse   past all faith   all faith   in any-

thing like that   and almost   in anything at all.   All-powerful al-
most. A period   that must stand   & decidedly so.   For now.

For another kind of stop   soon enough. But what to do   in the mean-
time   if not ok to just wait   since   that hasn't worked very well

so far has it   and why even ask the place or end of this?   I   I   do
not know   if it and its outrun panting is complicit.   But I   do

know that it's about all   I   know   to do. For now.   Sorry about that.
But there it is. Bonkaça? Byt here sic   & now   I dare say we   we have

something ahead of us   something like   a   ledger
or is it legend   something like a looming   and a long   unflexed atmos-

pheric

winter.

* * *

I celebrate the existence of the past in the mind   & call it
so. & Cull it   undistilled.   I celebrate   the existence of the past

in the mind and the radial boundaries beyond which   we
turn and continue   all that pellicule   rested there somehow   it is set

though like it   or not   and after all   you're   going to
have   to   you're going to have to   change   your life

into lives.   Such signals   nothing better than that

for now. Sit venia   but again and still   I celebrate the strange & stoney
existence of the past   in unmetaphorical folds of brain   or okay

fine of mind. Exclam. "…les êtres que j'ai perdus…" Agreement of prec-
edent object and post-conjugal participle   lesson one partially derived

from this particular curve of bench   plaqued w/ eroded memorial.   But let's not
get on with our enigmas just yet. Just room to stretch out and   scratch   a bit

just jut lips atop a bottle angled just so   and so the wind
outside sounds   today where we are   outside in that

hollow of glass   silly world-form on a hill. The voices press into it the vibr.
atory thing we both are and are in.   Ionization might

be it   I mean what we're waiting for   an instant.
aneous response across an underground network appar-

ently. It's hard to tell   in that scene   where   she bends over exhal.
ing cigarette smoke into the vulcanized   field of ancient corpse-pockets.

Pressing how hard depends on   how many lines & paths cork&screwed   into semblance
of everyday   something or other that must   change or get done first   plural done plural.

No agreement there. Just days and all they've been hiding
and tumbling forward in miracle of degringolating passion

persistent like all this in guts of mud. There too   the folds enfold hexag.
onally   as if the message.   Faint strains

of water and steam. There too   call it something it both is   and
is the container of: "your life." As if something at stake there also = X. This

"strange notion" that "things have happened" & have happened "to me."   Or   rather
to someone very nearby but who never quite   made it   to the party.   This accreted

mesh & its unanchored insistence   its
crushing nullity in voice of historical accident.

Question can a voice it.
self be crushed? Surely

but destruction   of   systematicity might be merely
its effacement in a brain   too worn   to manifest.

For if he rubs   he's a
rubber   isn't he? Of dust, of

rubble, that again. One after
another or mostly   all at

once.

                                                                But

there's a but but   that is not what this brain is begging   &least not yet.   A+ for
you   the entire back row.   Whereas in absence of   address   the

dire juncture lies here   in the ground of all their   faces &appeals
&   it's all oblique to me. And yet without that I/they would what-if

themselves into the most painful purgatory   or is it limbo I forget—
there where pain is said to consist primarily in distance and aperiod.

icity. In other words living   combustibly
                                                             but what if no

words for what then   .   None for now either   hence this manic pro.
cession. So many bottled breaths. So much must alcohol   reap.

praise, when ingested. Why did I have to smoke so much when I could breathe
oops meant to say   was young.   So odd to puzzle this now but that

really is where it all got started   bitter cigs stubbed in grass   al.
one mostly so far in nook of puddling stream &death cliff &we knew

we did we did   us kids   "cancer sticks" like nails no coffin
            but   still horizon   swallow its outsides and   render

it back into anonymous hacking through the walls   and can you not see
that   indelible compact of social class is the diamond scratching   a pane

dividing you from the goings on you have already renounced   and so we will
we will   not seek but heaven knows   events' nec. released   & unhindered

& riot-packed heads unbelieving drive on   in need of hiven   sic
and we   our algebra exhausted & in unresolve   yes we will

find you   we will   in specious caverns   in speech rodded and pulped
in pap of darkness   in newb. or suckle   in lock and hole of paper and

body   as though   with some final face I guess   as though   any step
were approxim. & stead   as though   any might   could unloose culmin.

ation   as though lone& enwebbed exper. on earth if cast into   phrase
        were   compens. & trust

enough   of all the rest

                                              as if.

III

Sententious

(dream notebook)

"Awareness is not always cognition."

The line grows longer, it is lunchtime.

A mask on even alone in a car with the windows rolled up.

"Overconfidence is a form of self-protection."

...screams in the elevator.

How sleep becomes a kind of furniture, bracing the day.

"Because heartbreak also breaks you open."

Sweaty underarms get in the way.

An object world where things no longer explain themselves.

"Culture war hides class war."

You can call it music this play that's not the Thing.

A hate letter to an empire in decline.

"I hope you're keeping some kind of record."

a special kind of everyday terror.

Incomplete

Ravening
and   the gloss attributed
to   rain on surfaces otherwise matte   under
      tain with   dolor and rose.
The trouble with isolation is that   distracting colosphere
by which   [_____]

Words feather through the blank texture of   rubbery
manila.

And the iris'd pearl of all this saying   next to nothing - -
as though rough be coughed over bough-bend and trough - -
         (jeez english is a tough dough to need)

&   the well-urned mind weren't dead, the eye   alone with
a place   in your   apostrophe.

Oaken stare and maple yellows of 4 p. m.

Having once cursed the shark of your latter day -
dreaming , the   murmur-bent colors of a quiet tale
on the grass, the sick waves of sleep behind
raw lids, submerging even this book, its
decadical waiting, unscrawled, its trolling spine.

Not loving poetry, but bodily something with
no other name —
spicturally,
motational,
unregraved

— in the absence of the absence of help   addressed to
whomsoever it mingth in nose or lash.

Rending, and the tissue made of glas
remains ready, functioning, formal
in the automatic deeps
the ancient school of   -spectation

a longing   in open sas of arrival:

slive of globe in enucleate orbital veinery.   But plz note:

These parabolae are not mad   just close-enough sembles of cross-charred redress.

And Now: the usual

Did any of it really happen?
Don't exactly know, and now the strange-
       shaped cloud
       and now the bubbles
                      skittering   popping
          atop the coffee
       [ask the hard questions: what is an object?]

and now the drum-thud waking   the pillow weighing
            out the light
            and now the summer less than a dream
the usual thickening = evaporation of somth
            never quite adding up
the usual   laughing wooden head turning
            mechanically on an axis too vertical
to credit.

           With an image on a screen I have
spoken, missing   as in true mathesis the one it shows,

ionized materialization   too ground-swollen

to admit

as though massive   pie-sections

of a life were   strained   by   spatial perspective

toward a point where evrythng

(itslf a   -thing)

really does   disappear as you watch — you too

My friend

with young white hair ,   your eternal city   and dwelling

which i have seen "in person" , your old youth   & mine

and all the negligent ages that surely could not

have been otherwise

[than negligent [I mean]

since for heaven's sake] who can keep up

with all that   flaking away

and what kind of life would have to have been nec.

in order   in order   to race   as we do

toward the end   can't help this

[telescopic doppler]

without such a wire twisting through

the pith and empty of it   without the raging

play of forces demanding now   and now

another life entirely another one   past

and   a past to tell of   only   in its
unruly ghosting   of eternity

it's just too bad   there's no time for all
that

Or that being dead in that way you already
have to be is to

be dead in   classic time-drenched dissolve   And nothing but
a sleepwalk in pine needles on a sap-stained hill   in summer
sol-

or   long x'd-out methexis   will   press through to burn
and through sea and through skin
all still blazing   and a stone-furnished cavern carpeted by tides
Tyrrhena and Adria   now so indifferent to our senile sprites
and now still   there's no summing up

this twice-ferried Split of them.

Imperative

Normally not in the afternoon.

Fixing squares and Christ
what kind of jinx must have
descended there
phases of Hum-
ankind   reduced
to this   blank
sequestered   waste   between
average rates of profit
and the interest fixed
on the dishes.

All to be washed.

There, in a place marked
Apartment of Beauty
and in   a rage of circulation
glove   equals hand equals mirror

equals face
it   that spectral recoop
it's never gonna
happen . . .

And yet has so mean it already. Single plural image. Rats.
To catch up to that evidence,
circumvent the imperative mode. Ditto below.

Tinny squeaks comb back blood   but go their way,
round round the bend
and curve like rope   the Brain.

Digest. Put output out.
Freeze forms in number
in genre. Dissolve the -ology
of winos. Be mad
at all this and yet
assimilate the syntax of the last century but one - -
or even better its dominant lack of mood.
Branlate and break it   down.
Bifurcolate.
Busy ranking several orders

of desert (*dē-**sert**)
windy needs continue the lead
of their contrivance.

Pocked and scarred
the advancing face of morning.

Reneg on direction
Braid hands
into mute knot of
broken gear   metallic prayer-like mumble
inbrothered   handle
as in   nickname   in gentle tease &
untrafficked sign of de facto belonging
so gentle too in cause as in   dreamt-of gig
& flash   (frog-wise light)
in cold wake of noontime   airs - -

risen to aigüe of grass blade   so literal
as to cut cut cut   this path of splintered paces

Except

Brine sides with Topic
and trundle. Such gesture
such awkward awk.
When will freezing non-winter
verge? Dirty word in another lang.
but there are no dirty words ex-
cept. 30 mins & 45 round - give
and take eyeglasses so close as
to reach edge of leaf right there. X now. But
no sea or time of it. Humble spot
and maculate, now again, over previous
unknown. Statue in block of blank.
Kind garden, and kinder, but too ancient
and unlearned even to heed this this much. And if
not exactly obscene all words are foreign,   after all.
Scream then clamber. Ignite then mow.
Where fog fits brain like orange and iso-
and like. Where day fits life like _____ . Where
open is what cannot both auto- and self-. Reduced
now to look and sound of running stop

light. Reduct. to expans. of idiot tub.
Of head & gut. Fire lit and sticking
whatever in it. Till break of n-other.
Till wait stays and topples,
cold head mumble dumbly
motocyc. Rails and mental drift. Eternal family
memb.'s on angel shoulder of Gold. On Wall-down
& Graffito. On boulder chip + Zip.
loc. now = tack & cork, Noted: 1988
& dream sweet dream of go-mad & die.

= = = = = = = = = = = = = = = =

Strides amid but Stop Gap.
Renard or requin, requine, but not alone.
Not yet and yet Enough but not Sufficient
to go on & chew into that.
So many remedies in any case.
Except. Severed through and even then.
Next throw will be prime and map
and lever. Then see these thoughts' curve
and stake their stimmig edges. Line through
and contin. and sleep. Tied under to flee

from one eye and cave. Grott. Flock. Knob-
Log & Logik sic broken and singed into mask
of lang. & sense. Sirens and poop. Inverted deck
of perspect. Step armed into storm of bone. All gnarl
lifted and unmet gun. Stop nugget stop engine. Reap
catastr. but only betw. of Read. Brought to you
by pack and Packers. Morsel beaded & sown
dispersed as seeded cries into troughs of intensity
slips of hungered ache   glut of foam steam brume & wave.

creux de concentration

What if rule – reglement and right – were to write with one thick thought

for knead

("idea"? "god forbid"?) and   not

when mere   least cast

of blank   in stead // in stand

unlike   when write   *in order to*   blank   both

up to now   cause unknown // empty   page   +

so often so   ring in   ear

//

— to make vibration that will make vibr. & stop —

//

Need make move   who knows

some *matter*   which   one

just stewing

Press   and rave   or rather   around?

on stuff /

    / "in there"   just clogging

                              up

or better   tadpoles

      crawling   out of

           water

                running over

Q can one crawl   mounds

    in lack of all

      appendage?

        You see   generation

          auto-   of articul-

If instead   gen   ate field

   principle of   -eration   on bas-

were to   be the   is of

lie   so

  in   active germ   its quandering

    & yeast   lay

 in-   taken form

   as of concipit

    non-conquerit   + ecstat. & recept.

& heeding   all-around

    nervous shimmer   world of Spring

                                & dying

    par ex. &   leaf/skin

all inter-communic.   &   footprint in side-

all-heaving   & cruel   walk   or dog-

    means   in return   of   shit   even

                        etern.   e.g.

— sneeze too a gift of endless time & a frosty aftern. sun —

What then

    -to concl.-   the yard   little

    if   the things of   tufty   rect.

    &   angle

    the meeting   here

    faces   in traffic

                         in cash

What were it   sect.   (digit.)

    but   inter-   aband.

on edge

where too

but a sweep of time be needed ?

— Patterns in the marble   couched & layered —

unauthored epic   crested mane

join of senseless plan/et

of unstolen earth   &

fine-ground bones   of

us all   —

Reward and rain, separate //
Bi-level sections of strenuous //
Remind but don't rememb. //
Resolution peaks just past, just over

Brown waves, and foam dissociate (adj.//pron. as noun)

Rectilinear patterns apparently and really

Rhomboid, a ruse of static, a price
not quite determined in the manner of your long-bearded
uncle's internal exile, whereas the silence per-
taining to its conditions rattles into shape, finally,
in unremarked self-concert. By way of
pseudo-contradictions the falling chaff leads
our gaze softly to   solar remnants of
its insufficient gravity. Next time the arch will
be several degrees meaner, but all the more
inviting, as it bends toward the Thing we
keep locked in the cellar. What if you
were to name the shape of temporal structures

by shouting stuff like Football or We're
out of syrup   or   Don't cry you can play now?
My dresses fit over them with equal precision.

Is that how space contracts to ten to the
negative one millionth in this index of cleverness
or would it be better to think of it as the
ego getting the relief it needs for free   while
all the rest of us   have to remove our shoes
by the door ? No one has ever arrived at
such fruitful conclusions with so little
effort or aesthetic scruple, unless it be
the janitor in the hall   used to being more or
less   ignored   or the shady interests behind
proposals for dial tones that didn't make the
cut.
Now we have pads for that, saying unselved. Just follow the law
to the letter even if it be by nature
incommensurate with phenomena as such
and boy do I know it is. Shocking isn't
it to realize how many alternate forms of
every force N there is are   will ever be   Even the
police have trouble with this and they still

just say "hang up" when other more menacing
locutions strain to worm through. So fuck all that. So
all these rhythms end, unpenetrated by
the knowledge of their schemes and aims
however projectively inherent   however
indubitably rigged   the race set off   oh sweet jesus
it looks   like   looks like   forever

Afterword

The poems in this collection were first written some years ago. Before Trump, before Covid, before George Floyd, before January 6, to name only the most salient metonymic markers of recent crises. Also at an earlier point in the ever more massive, widespread and frequent climate disruptions of each passing year (most of us had never seen the California sky darkened orange with smoke until September of 2020—and as I write this, Canada smolders, Hawaii burns. . .). I feel it important to signal this chronology, given the turbulence of these years and the relative lack of identifiable allusions in this work to any of the recent large scale events that have concerned us all. I say relative in part because, while the poems were written earlier, they were typed up and revised much more recently, and the staggered timing of that process has marked them here and there as well. But I say relative also because whatever urgency is voiced here—in a language of breakdown that is already oblique, at a loss, in disarray with respect to it own histories—lies in deep continuity with the many ills that have come so spectacularly into the foreground over this period. The problems in view have intensified, become more pointed, but at bottom they are not essentially new. That long and jagged continuity, carved across one dismembered voice or rather set of voices traversing its/their own singular trajectory, along with the multi-layered disorder thereby witnessed, is one of the primary tonal addresses proffered by these poems—themselves drawn from long-filled notebooks that have called out more and more for a less lonely life outside their scrawled-on pages. One exception to this is the opening poem, keyboard-composed specifically for this book one grey East Bay morning in August of 2023.

The references to Kafka and blackness were inspired by *Kafka's Blues: Figurations of Racial Blackness in the Construction of an Aesthetic*, by Mark Christian Thompson.

Many many thanks to Atopon Books for believing in this work and guiding it into existence as a book.